It is N.... ı ork in the year 2030. What is different in this future? Well, there are new planes, flying cars, many tall buildings, and astronauts can travel to Mars. But some things are not so different from today . . .

People watch the news on television and go to cafés. People have computers and use e-mail. And it is not a good future for everybody – there are still many hungry and poor people in America . . . and all over the world. And there is killing, too.

Computerhead wants to change things and make a better future for everybody. But how do you help people and make them happy. There are good ways and bad ways. And doing the right thing is not always easy.

OXFORD BOOKWORMS LIBRARY

Fantasy & Horror

New York Café

Starter (250 headwords)

MICHAEL DEAN

New York Café

Illustrated by
Peter Richardson

OXFORD UNIVERSITY PRESS

OXFORD
UNIVERSITY PRESS

Great Clarendon Street, Oxford OX2 6DP

Oxford University Press is a department of the University of Oxford.
It furthers the University's objective of excellence in research, scholarship,
and education by publishing worldwide in

Oxford New York

Auckland Cape Town Dar es Salaam Hong Kong Karachi
Kuala Lumpur Madrid Melbourne Mexico City Nairobi
New Delhi Shanghai Taipei Toronto

With offices in

Argentina Austria Brazil Chile Czech Republic France Greece
Guatemala Hungary Italy Japan Poland Portugal Singapore
South Korea Switzerland Thailand Turkey Ukraine Vietnam

OXFORD and OXFORD ENGLISH are registered trade marks of
Oxford University Press in the UK and in certain other countries

ISBN: 978 0 19 423423 8

A complete recording of this Bookworms edition of
New York Café is available on audio CD. ISBN 978 0 19 423405 4

Printed in China

Word count (main text): 1570

For more information on the Oxford Bookworms Library, visit
www.oup.com/bookworms

CONTENTS

AUGUST 15 2030 It is August 15, 2030, and an e-mail from S. Fuller is going to Computer 1 at the First Bank of New York. It says, 'Take one cent from 5,000,000 people and give it all to S. Fuller. Then forget this e-mail.' Nobody at the office of the First Bank of New York sees the e-mail. It goes into the computer, the computer gives the money to S. Fuller and then it forgets the e-mail. After that, the e-mail is not in the computer, and only S. Fuller knows about it.

1

AUGUST 16   The Fuller family is looking at the family's
2030   money on their computer.

'There's $50,000 more in the bank, now,' says Mr Fuller.

'But, Simon, why?' asks Mrs Fuller. 'Why $50,000 more?'

'I don't know,' says Mr Fuller.

Sam, the son, smiles.

'It's good!' he says. 'Don't ask questions about it. Be happy!'

'I'm not happy about it,' says Mr Fuller. 'Because I don't understand it.'

'Who wants a drink?' says Sheila, Sam's little sister.

AUGUST 17 The e-mail from S. Fuller to New York Café **2 0 3 0** says, 'I can take money from the bank with my computer and give it to my dad. But I need to do much more. I want to help people and make them happy. I am very, very good with computers – the best in New York. How can I help people? Maybe I can help people with no money. Can somebody at the New York Café help me?'

The e-mail from New York Café to S. Fuller begins like this, 'This is New York Café and my name is Computerhead. At this computer café we are all good with computers. We can do lots of things with computers here. Do you want to help people? People with no money? I like that! OK. I can help you. You must . . . '

3

AUGUST 18 Two astronauts are going to Mars. But **2030** suddenly one of them says, 'Hey, the computer's taking us back to New York. We're not going to Mars. We're going back home. I can't stop this computer!'

AUGUST 18 One of the astronauts says, 'What's that?
2030 An e-mail?' The e-mail to the astronauts says, 'Do not go to Mars. It does not help poor people. It does not make them happy. I can stop your computers again. And again and again. So give $1,000,000,000 to people with no money TODAY and then tell the television people. I want it on the news!'

AUGUST 19 The next day, the Fuller family watch the **2030** news on television. The news-reader is saying, 'Two astronauts are back in New York. Something's wrong with the computer . . . ' There is a picture of the astronauts and a picture of the computer. But there is nothing on television about $1,000,000,000 for people with no money.

AUGUST 20 A plane is going from New York to **2030** London. But then suddenly the plane's computer stops it. The plane waits over New York. It gets an e-mail message. 'All the people on this plane have a lot of money. Give some of your money to poor people by e-mail, now. Then you can go to London.'

AUGUST 21 Some very important people are talking in
2030 New York.

'Who's doing this to the computers?'

'We don't know.'

'Well, we must find him. How can we find him?'

'We're looking for a signal, from his computer. Every
computer has a signal. When we find the signal, we find
him.'

'OK. But I tell you this: He must stop now. Do you understand?'

'Well, we can give a new password to all the important computers in the country. And without a computer's password he can't get into the computer.'

'OK. Give new passwords to all the important computers in America. At the same time, find the signal from **his** computer. But most important, find him!'

AUGUST 22   S. Fuller e-mails Computerhead at New
2030   York Café and says, 'I am not happy. The
police are putting new passwords in all the important
computers in America. I cannot get into them. I do not
want to stop now. Computerhead, help me!'

AUGUST 23
2030 The e-mail from Computerhead at New York Café to S. Fuller says, 'Fuller no, please do not stop your work. I am an old man now. I do not know you, but I have a picture of you in my head. I see a young man. What are you, seventeen or eighteen years old? And you want to do something good! OK! Let's do something very good! I can help you. Let's talk again tomorrow.'

AUGUST 24 **2030** Today's e-mail from Computerhead to S. Fuller says, 'I am sending you a box. It can help you. When you send a signal to any computer, it finds the computer's password. And then you are in the computer and you can do anything with it. Any computer in America is your computer. Let's talk again tomorrow.'

AUGUST 25
2 0 3 0 Computerhead sends S. Fuller an e-mail. It says, 'Fuller, there is one more thing. The police are looking for your computer signal. From now on, send everything by e-mail to me at New York Café. Later I can send it out again from here, with a lot of new signals. Then, they cannot find your signal. Fuller, tomorrow is an important day for you.'

AUGUST 26 The next e-mail from Computerhead to
2030 S. Fuller says, 'Fuller, this man's name is
Smith. You must get his computer password. But get his
computer password at home, not at work. It is easy. I
know this man because I work with him. What is his work?
He kills people.'

AUGUST 26 Another e-mail from Computerhead to S.
2030 Fuller says, 'Yes, Smith kills people. And I help him. But now I am doing something good, for the first time. Tomorrow you and I can help poor people. Tomorrow we can do something big. Tomorrow people must listen to us. We want a new America, Fuller. A new America!'

AUGUST 26 Mr and Mrs Fuller are very happy, but the
2 0 3 0 children are not.

'Hey, we're going sailing for two weeks,' says Mr Fuller.

'Oh no!' says Sam. 'I want to stay here.'

'Me too,' says his little sister, Sheila.

'But why, Sam?' says Mrs Fuller.

'Mum, I'm eighteen. I have important things to do,' says
Sam.

'Important things? What important things?' says Mr
Fuller.

'I can't tell you that,' says Sam.

'Oh, Simon, it's OK,' says Mrs Fuller. 'You and I can go.
The children can stay here.'

'OK,' says Mr Fuller. But he is angry and leaves the room.

AUGUST 27 The e-mail from S. Fuller to Computerhead
2030 at New York Café says, 'My mum and dad
are sailing now. I have more time at the computer. Mr
Smith's password is his daughter's name. I am in Smith's
computer now. He works in Washington. I am going into
the President's computer. I can do a lot of things now. Look
at the next picture!'

17

AUGUST 27
2030
S. Fuller sends the President an e-mail. It says, 'Dear Mr President. Look at this picture. The missiles can stay in the sky or they can come down. I can bring them down with my computer. Are you listening to me, Mr President? I want a better America. I do not want money. Not for me. I want money for poor people. And sandwiches. Give sandwiches to poor people. Start now, or they all come down tomorrow.'

AUGUST 27   The President has S. Fuller's e-mail and he
2030   is very angry.

'Sandwiches! Sandwiches! Can we stop this? Please?'

'No, Mr President. I'm sorry. We can't find the signal.'

'What do we do now?'

'Give money to poor people, Mr President. Make sandwiches. Do anything for now. We need more time.'

'OK. You! Yes, you. The tall man in the white shirt. Go and make some sandwiches.'

'Yes, Mr President.'

AUGUST 27 A woman is running into the President's
2 0 3 0   office.

'Mr President,' says the woman. 'We have his signal. It's coming from a computer café in New York.'

'OK!' says the President. 'Get him!'

AUGUST 27 'A better America. I want a better America,'
2030 says Computerhead. The police take him
away. Then they look at his computer at the New York
Café. There is an e-mail there. It is from S. Fuller.

AUGUST 27
2030 The police have Sam now, too. Sam is very afraid. He says, 'Stop! I must phone my mum and dad. They're sailing. And my little sister's here. I can't leave her. Why are you doing this? Please stop.'

AUGUST 28
2030
Mr and Mrs Fuller are with their son. They are talking to the police.

'Sam?' says Mrs Fuller. 'Our Sam and this . . . Computerhead? Sorry, but I must laugh.'

'It's not our Sam,' says Mr Fuller. 'Sam can't understand computers. His teachers help him, but he's no good.'

'Yes,' says Mrs Fuller. 'Sheila helps him too. Sheila's very good with computers.'

'Oh yes,' says Mr Fuller. 'Sheila's the best girl in New York with computers.'

Mr Fuller looks at Mrs Fuller and then Mrs Fuller looks at Mr Fuller.

'Where's Sheila?' say Mr and Mrs Fuller.

AUGUST 28 S. Fuller's last e-mail to Computerhead **2030** says, 'Hello. Where are you? My e-mails to you come back all the time. Can you see the picture? Look at the missiles, in the Washington sky. They are going to New York, London, Tokyo, Paris, Moscow and Rome too. But I cannot get them down, Computerhead. Can you help me? What do I do now?'

GLOSSARY

bank you put your money in a bank, but you can have it
  when you want it again

Mars it is up in the sky; it is red

maybe perhaps

news a TV programme that tells about things that happen

news-reader someone who reads the news

password a number or word you use for opening a
  computer

poor people with no money or very little money are poor

president the most important man or woman in America,
  the first president of the United States was George
  Washington

sailing going through water on a boat

send you can write to a friend with a pen and send it or you
  can send your friend an e-mail from your computer to her
  or his computer

signal every computer leaves a mark or signal when it sends
  a message

New York Café

ACTIVITIES

Before Reading

1 **Look at the picture on the cover of the book. Now answer these questions.**

1 Which word is important for the story? Choose one answer.

a ☐ cars
b ☐ computers
c ☐ planes

2 What do you think?
For each sentence choose one answer.

                                                 YES NO

a) The story is about a young boy or girl who is very good at computers. ☐ ☐

b) The story says 'Computers are more important than people.' ☐ ☐

c) The story says 'Be careful with computers.' ☐ ☐

2 **Read the back cover of the book. For each sentence choose one answer.**

1 The story happens in
a) ☐ America. b) ☐ Britain. c) ☐ your country.

2 The end of the story is
a) ☐ happy. b) ☐ not happy. c) ☐ not a or b.

ACTIVITIES

————————

While Reading

1 Read pages 1–3, then answer these questions.

1 How much money does S. Fuller get from the First Bank of New York?

2 What does the computer do with the e-mail after it gives the money to S. Fuller?

3 Who knows about S. Fuller's e-mail to the bank?

2 Read pages 4–7, then answer these questions.

Who . . . ?

1 . . . is going to Mars and then goes back home?

2 . . . sees the astronauts on television?

3 . . . gets an e-mail saying 'Give some of your money to poor people.'

3 Read pages 8–12. Are these sentences true (T) or false (F)?

	T	F
1 All the computers in America get new passwords.	☐	☐
2 S. Fuller needs Computerhead's help with the new passwords.	☐	☐
3 Computerhead is a young man.	☐	☐
4 S. Fuller gives Computerhead a box that can find a computer's password.	☐	☐

4 Read pages 13–16 and answer these questions.

1 Who is looking for S. Fuller's computer signal?
2 Where must S. Fuller send all e-mails now?
3 What does Smith do?
4 Who goes to the sea for two weeks and who stays at home?

5 Read pages 17–20. Who says or thinks these words?

1 'I can do a lot of things.'
2 'Look at this! He can bring missiles down with his computer.'
3 'Yes, Mr President.'
4 'We have his signal.'

6 Before you read pages 21–24, guess which of these happens.

1 ☐ The police find Computerhead at the Computer Café and take him away.
2 ☐ The police do not find Computerhead but he and S. Fuller do not send the missiles.
3 ☐ The police find S. Fuller before S. Fuller sends the missiles to Washington.
4 ☐ The police find S. Fuller only after S. Fuller sends the missiles to Washington (and more cities).

After Reading

1 Put these sentences in the right order.

a ☐ Mr and Mrs Fuller go to the sea.

b ☐ S. Fuller sends all his e-mails to the New York Café.

c ☐ S. Fuller sends an e-mail to the astronauts.

d ☐ Important computers have new passwords.

e ☐ The First Bank of New York gives $5,000 to Mr Fuller.

f ☐ The police find Computerhead.

g ☐ S. Fuller gets into Smith's computer.

h ☐ Computerhead helps S. Fuller find the new passwords.

i ☐ S. Fuller sends an e-mail to a plane.

j ☐ The police find S. Fuller.

k ☐ S. Fuller and Computerhead send missiles into the sky.

2 You are S. Fuller. Send a last e-mail to Computerhead.

'Hello. There is something I must tell you. My name is . . .'

....

....

....

....

....

3 **Look at each picture, then answer the questions after it.**

1

Who are these people?
What are they doing?
What are they wearing?

2

Where is this?
Who are the people?
What are they doing?

3

Where is this?
What is happening?

ABOUT THE AUTHOR

Michael Dean worked for many years as a teacher and lecturer of English. He is now a full-time writer and lives in the east of England. He has written many textbooks and stories for English learners all over the world. For the Oxford Bookworms Library he has written *A Ghost in Love and Other Plays* (Stage 1, Playscripts).

OXFORD BOOKWORMS LIBRARY

Classics • Crime & Mystery • Factfiles • Fantasy & Horror
Human Interest • Playscripts • Thriller & Adventure
True Stories • World Stories

The OXFORD BOOKWORMS LIBRARY provides enjoyable reading in English, with a wide range of classic and modern fiction, non-fiction, and plays. It includes original and adapted texts in seven carefully graded language stages, which take learners from beginner to advanced level. An overview is given on the next pages.

All Stage 1 titles are available as audio recordings, as well as over eighty other titles from Starter to Stage 6. All Starters and many titles at Stages 1 to 4 are specially recommended for younger learners. Every Bookworm is illustrated, and Starters and Factfiles have full-colour illustrations.

The OXFORD BOOKWORMS LIBRARY also offers extensive support. Each book contains an introduction to the story, notes about the author, a glossary, and activities. Additional resources include tests and worksheets, and answers for these and for the activities in the books. There is advice on running a class library, using audio recordings, and the many ways of using Oxford Bookworms in reading programmes. Resource materials are available on the website <www.oup.com/bookworms>.

The *Oxford Bookworms Collection* is a series for advanced learners. It consists of volumes of short stories by well-known authors, both classic and modern. Texts are not abridged or adapted in any way, but carefully selected to be accessible to the advanced student.

You can find details and a full list of titles in the *Oxford Bookworms Library Catalogue* and *Oxford English Language Teaching Catalogues*, and on the website <www.oup.com/bookworms>.

STARTER • 250 HEADWORDS

present simple – present continuous – imperative –
can/cannot, must – *going to* (future) – simple gerunds …

Her phone is ringing – but where is it?

Sally gets out of bed and looks in her bag. No phone. She looks under the bed. No phone. Then she looks behind the door. There is her phone. Sally picks up her phone and answers it. *Sally's Phone*

STAGE 1 • 400 HEADWORDS

… past simple – coordination with *and*, *but*, *or* –
subordination with *before*, *after*, *when*, *because*, *so* …

I knew him in Persia. He was a famous builder and I worked with him there. For a time I was his friend, but not for long. When he came to Paris, I came after him – I wanted to watch him. He was a very clever, very dangerous man. *The Phantom of the Opera*

STAGE 2 • 700 HEADWORDS

… present perfect – *will* (future) – *(don't) have to, must not, could* –
comparison of adjectives – simple *if* clauses – past continuous –
tag questions – *ask/tell* + infinitive …

While I was writing these words in my diary, I decided what to do. I must try to escape. I shall try to get down the wall outside. The window is high above the ground, but I have to try. I shall take some of the gold with me – if I escape, perhaps it will be helpful later. *Dracula*

... should, may – present perfect continuous – *used to* – past perfect –
causative – relative clauses – indirect statements ...

Of course, it was most important that no one should see
Colin, Mary, or Dickon entering the secret garden. So Colin
gave orders to the gardeners that they must all keep away
from that part of the garden in future. ***The Secret Garden***

... past perfect continuous – passive (simple forms) –
would conditional clauses – indirect questions –
relatives with *where/when* – gerunds after prepositions/phrases ...

I was glad. Now Hyde could not show his face to the world
again. If he did, every honest man in London would be proud
to report him to the police. ***Dr Jekyll and Mr Hyde***

... future continuous – future perfect –
passive (modals, continuous forms) –
would have conditional clauses – modals + perfect infinitive ...

If he had spoken Estella's name, I would have hit him. I was so
angry with him, and so depressed about my future, that I could
not eat the breakfast. Instead I went straight to the old house.
Great Expectations

... passive (infinitives, gerunds) – advanced modal meanings –
clauses of concession, condition

When I stepped up to the piano, I was confident. It was as if I
knew that the prodigy side of me really did exist. And when I
started to play, I was so caught up in how lovely I looked that
I didn't worry how I would sound. ***The Joy Luck Club***

Starman

PHILLIP BURROWS AND MARK FOSTER

The empty centre of Australia. The sun is hot and there are not many people. And when Bill meets a man, alone, standing on an empty road a long way from anywhere, he is surprised and worried.

And Bill is right to be worried. Because there is something strange about the man he meets. Very strange . . .

Vampire Killer

PAUL SHIPTON

'I am a vampire killer . . . and now I need help,' says Professor Fletcher to Colin. Colin needs a job and he needs money but do vampires exist or is the professor crazy?

A Connecticut Yankee in King Arthur's Court

MARK TWAIN

Retold by Alan Hines

Hank Morgan is a happy young man in Connecticut, USA in 1879 until one day someone runs into his office and shouts, 'Come quickly, Boss! Two men are fighting.' After this, something very strange happens to him, and his life changes forever.

The White Stones

LESTER VAUGHAN

'The people on this island don't like archaeologists,' the woman on the ferry says. You only want to study the 4,500 year-old Irish megalithic stones but very soon strange things begin to happen to you. Can you solve the mystery in time?

Under the Moon

ROWENA AKINYEMI

It is the year 2522, and the planet Earth is dying. The Artificial Ozone Layer is only 300 years old, but it is breaking up fast. Now the sun is burning down on Earth with a white fire. There is no water. Without water, nothing can live. Trees die, plants die, animals die, people die . . .

In a colony under the moon, people wait for news – news from home, news from the planet Earth. And in a spaceship high above Earth, a young man watches numbers on a computer screen. The numbers tell a story, and the young man is afraid.

The planet Earth is burning, burning, burning . . .

A Ghost in Love and Other Plays

MICHAEL DEAN

Do you believe in ghosts? The characters in these three original plays don't. The first is set in the seventeenth century, and the other two take place in modern times. In each play, a ghost comes back from the dead to change the lives of living people.